J. Marion Sims, the legendary, gynecologist looms large in Bettii Sophisticated, complex, haunting, *Patient.* beckons readers to remember, to feel, to think deeply, to discover, to probe. Slavery's stench, the bodies of Black women, death, scientific racism, memory—these themes link the poems in extraordinary ways. Judd is a masterful new poet. *Patient.* is unforgettable!!

—**Beverly Guy-Sheftall, Founding Director and Anna Julia Cooper Professor of Women's Studies, Spelman College**

In *Patient.* Bettina Judd beautifully (and horrifically) draws on historical evidence of nineteenth-century medical experimentation on black women, scholarly explorations of the body and the archive, and personal medical history. The result is haunting in its insistence on laying bare these stories as they not only articulate experiences of the past but also resonate deeply with black women's experiences with the U.S. medical complex in the present. *Patient.* is a brilliant meditation on race, gender, and science and a thrilling anthem to black women's self-knowledge.

—**Elsa Barkley Brown, Associate Professor of History and Women's Studies, University of Maryland, College Park**

Joice Heth. Lucy Zimmerman. Betsey Harris. Anarcha Wescott. Bettina Judd ensures you will remember the names of four women assaulted by science, violated by curiosity—survivors of physical invasion and torturous experiments. She presents their dignity, heretofore denied, as imagined in their own voices in conversation and parallel with a modern speaker, similarly (coldly) ensnared by a medical machine powered by detachment at best, cruelty at worst. Judd re-centers the narrative, however, to where it belongs—on the person(s) confronted, examined, in pain—not on the problem to be studied or solved. In visceral language that indicts, worships, haunts, and empowers, *Patient.* illuminates "a dynasty, a bloodline, a body" imbued with the full human spectrum of emotion and brilliance.

—**Khadijah Queen, author of *Conduit* and *Black Peculiar***

patient.

poems

Bettina Judd

Black
Lawrence
Press

Black
Lawrence
Press

www.blacklawrence.com

Executive Editor: Diane Goettel
Book and Cover Design: Amy Freels
Cover Art: *How Much Does It Hurt? 1* by Bettina Judd

Published 2014 by Black Lawrence Press.
Printed in the United States.

CONTENTS

meaning is the river
of voices. meaning
is the patience of the moon.
meaning is the thread
running forever in shadow.

—Lucille Clifton

IN 2006 I HAD AN ORDEAL WITH MEDICINE.

I must have been found guilty of something. I don't *feel* innocent here lurking with ghosts. See   it happens like that. I start at a thought that is quite benign and end up peccant, debased.

I had an ordeal with medicine and was found innocent or guilty. It feels the same because I live in a haunted house. A house can be a dynasty, a bloodline, a body.

There was punishment.   Like the way the body is murdered by its own weight when lynched.   Not that I was wrong but that verdicts come in a bloodline.

In 2006 I had an ordeal with medicine. To recover, I learn why ghosts come to me. The research question is: Why am I patient?

Pathology.

THE RESEARCHER DISCOVERS ANARCHA, BETSEY, LUCY

> *Nurses ask me,*
> *"How much does it hurt on a scale from one to ten?"*

Anarcha Wescott, Betsey Harris, and Lucy Zimmerman are taken into the care of a reluctant country surgeon in Montgomery, Alabama.

> *see blood on a white hospital sheet,*
> *tell me I am having menstrual cramps*

Betsy's first birth,

> *send me home with oxycodone, ibuprofen*

Lucy, months out of household duties,

> *after five hours in triage*

Anarcha, his first vesico-vaginal fistula

> *and another prescription*

In these three, Sims shapes his speculum, invents his silver sutures, perfects protocol for proper handling of the female pelvis.

> *we wake*

Unanesthesized or addicted to opium, children born, children disappeared. Helpless   help.

THE RESEARCHER PRESENTS JOICE HETH

The curiosity that is

    every

black woman   blind, one paralyzed arm

    doctor

profitable bones, old breasts   some

    students in tow

wish they could suck   that they too would become
great men

    each to their own speculum.

Like any other curiosity, upon her death she will be
dissected.

SHEDDING
February 10, 2006

I had the urge to scoot out of my hips but there was no blood. The smell of it but nothing. I waited until there was, until the feeling stopped. By morning I was still waiting.

The doctor tells me that cramps are contractions of the uterus. *This is why they hurt, you know?*

I am shedding something. All night I wait for his oxycodone to work, pick a scab. *This is why they hurt, you know?*

HOW TO MEASURE PAIN I

In the woman it is a checklist:

Can you imagine anything
worse than this?

If the answer is no, ask again.

INITIATION/MEMORY
Late Evening February 16, 2006

Gynecology was built on the backs of Black women, anyway.

Hospital curtain, showman's speculum, surgeon's auditorium. There is an opening here, a thrusting, a climax, a little death.   Who will rise from that, and how? Why not stay dead and forget? Why do I choose to remember? You, in bed with me Anarcha. You, brushing my head Joice. Why do you mourn me and sing, as if I am the one who has died?

AFTER MEMORY

i keep on remembering mine.
—Lucille Clifton

It's like when a black person says: "that's racist!" to a white person and they refuse to believe. Maybe it is better to say, "This moment is steeped in a racist history. This racist history is indelibly printed on my memory. You do not want to remember, so you wish to erase mine." But it is not heard. One only hears what one hopes not to be, and that's racist.

After memory, I am absent. No table. No one on all fours. No children living or otherwise. No hymns. No nursemaids. No sideshow freaks. No experiments. No spoon. No bent handle, no wincing. Just whiskey, opium and: *Now, wasn't there some good?*

SUICIDE OF 100,000 ITS

J. Marion Sims narrates a case of infant lockjaw in his autobiography: "It had been in spasms for two days and nights, and looked as if it were dying. [...] touching it would throw it into convulsions; laying it on its face would cause spasms; any noise would produce them. It could not swallow, could take no nourishment, and it was impossible for it to suck. It was covered with a cold, clammy perspiration; its hands were tightly clinched, so that the finger-nails were almost cutting into the flesh on the palms of its hands. [...] as a matter of course, the child died. The next day we held a post-mortem examination."

Dear Doctor,

Go to the source of suffering. This is why I could not grow, why I would not eat, why I cut into my own flesh, refused to be touched. This is why I crawled inside myself and died—as a matter of course.

YOU BE LUCY, I'LL BE BETSEY
February 17, 2006

The nurse with the natural compliments me on my locs. We begin in that nappy-hair banter, *when did you start yours?* All of this happening between my thighs. Between speculum and cotton swab, *I just had to stop running to the salon.* Between the manual test in the vagina, *You're going to feel a pinch,* and the manual test in the anus, *It's so much easier to manage this way.* Nothing said of my outburst. Nothing about the angry patient on this floor, *Yours look so healthy,* nothing about why she tends to me after that. *Almost done.* Just two black women and a speculum, each asking the other, *When did you get free?*

IN SPECIAL COLLECTIONS,
A RITUAL OF ANGER

"The negro is a beast but created with articulate speech, and hands, that he may be of service to his master—the white man."
   —The Negro A Beast Or In The Image Of God
      by Charles Carroll

Another finding becomes a feeling: a medium between this and my mother's anger. Science and the ghost's exhale.   Another finding becomes a feeling: God   and the idea of God's absence. There is a spiral here, a sadness. Who would lay hands? Why would they if God is dead? Whom would they be in service to? Another finding becomes a feeling: there is no negro. No white man. Then what would hold us here? Another finding becomes feeling: she is in the page. I am turning myself.

PATHOLOGY

*noun. 1. sorrows sufferings 2. the branch of knowledge that deals
with the emotions. 3. the study of disease*
—Oxford English Dictionary

Or an easy diagnosis: Third world, ghetto, housing
project. Among the symptoms are shadows of the point
of contract: work camp, shanty town, the rez. To no
longer suffer, but exist.

Or:

Q. How are you, grandmother?
A. Fair to middlin'.

NEGATIVE SPACE METHODOLOGY[1]

The way they bend into my body, an easiness, closeness that makes this inquiry possible. Low hum, laughter, the sound of them folding back. Something familiar I want to learn yet cannot wake up early enough to watch my grandmother bake.

They will be found in their movement. Their hands in the cracks. Inhaling his breath, exhaling mine.

INNER TRUTH[2]

History is also everybody talking at once.[3] When I open my mouth, there is another voice. I have to press a finger to one tragus to hear me. The other becomes louder, more rapid. There are many voices now—gaps, garbled underwater talk, some of it in another language. Collected words: *pewter, automaton, john hopkin* string a line across my tongue. None of it is true.   All of it is true.

Use.

THE INAUGURATION OF EXPERIMENTS
December 1845

Lucy didn't scream like most. Though sometimes she would moan—deep, long and overdue. I'd wake thinking death. It's her, knees curled under, head face down, her body trying to move out of itself. Anarcha and I take turns wiping her head with cool rags, warming her feet with our hands, singing to her. She would join in a voice so low it wasn't like she was singing at all but whispering a prayer that hushed on long after we finished.

Doctor spent a lot of time with Lucy. He would stand at the foot of her bed looking. Not mad   just like he had a whole lot of questions and wanted answers from her. I had questions too, so I looked to Anarcha.

She thought a long time.   Finally said, *She too sick to die. We too well to be living.*

BETSEY'S HEAD RESTING ON PALMS[4]

Spirit flees the body and
its treacherous
tearing

Eyes land on nothing
ambling across a line
a scar

When I bring them low
it is to him and
the spoon

Tongue flicking, mouth gaping
I feel myself opening and
can no longer see

WHAT WE ARE MADE OF
~Betsey

No one ever asked me if I could make nothing before. Seems like it's just enough being made. Doctor Harris would put things in my hand for cleaning looked like they was for opening things made to stay shut. Metal, strange shaped, sometimes familiar like a knife or a spoon. I put on a deep pot of water, and when it start to make tiny bubbles on the sides I set, whatever it is, down, watch it turn into water bending and wobbling with the bluh bluh bluh sounds. Everything look the same silver and white, then brown. My face be water too.

ANARCHA TO THE SLOW BORN CHILD[5]

On the third day God planted seeds
After that, created sun and moon
sowed a reluctant harvest in me
a stubborn stalk that grew to know
there is nothing here for you

Littlegirl, what I do
looks like madness
But if I stay there would be
another kind of sloughing
Tired parts of humanity
falling away from each other

Exhaustion holds the heart
from screaming
tearing this way,
is soundless

Fold into me tight
forgive the soft parts
of your mother

WAIT

I squat babies
fling them on my back
our afterbirth fertilizer.

She, with me on quiet nights
a short-lived
forever love
made by the stink of us.

Doe stands over
her young.

Tree drops
sweetest fruit.

Snake slides away
from her own
delectable eggs.

I wish for pungent ether
settle for my own.

ETYMOLOGY OF ANARCHA I

from the term anarchy *meaning*
1. absence or denial of any authority or established order.
2. absence of order see disorder.

When the tearing came there was
no baby in the canal but a new route:

fistula, with a hard f like fetal
freak, fatal, furor.

I needed the f when the break screamed
no sound from me but fire, fuchsia

Becoming an un-fuckable woman, freedom
the black hole[6] of my sex, fare

to the good doctor I will be flesh
which you will think brutal

but I will be   finally

YOU COULD SMELL IT FROM THE FIELDS

A yellow brown of
open insides in heat
Mister Wescott keep away
everyone do.

Before little girl was born
preacher talked about a woman
had the nerve
to grab the hem of His garments.

I know now she wasn't
trying to be healed,
just wanted to reach for something
didn't mind her touch.

USE
~ Lucy

If I promise
will you get rid of her? I ask
wanting to be his
though I already was.

He filled my belly
ain't ask me nothing
bout her while I grew.

Baby girl stalled, I quieted
broke into many pieces.
Then I was useless
for days and days.

ETYMOLOGY OF ANARCHA II

A name for a ripe woman
pluckable and free

Stream of children
running between her legs

or perhaps, none.

I didn't want to go back. Not just to be cured but to never have to take the train again. Mister Z cackled said I won't run since he don't need a bloodhound to track my scent.

The car had crates and a floor for chairs. If I were to sit I would saturate myself more.   A jolt flung me into the lap of a man who smelled it and tossed me into the movement of the train. I hit the floor and the dark spot began to expand. He snarled something about how filthy women be.

I smoothed my dress. So not to trap his disgust inside.

PUT TOGETHER
~ Betsey

Ain't it possible to love a man? Not for jumping the broom because I can't be given to nobody. Not away. I wanted the wedding to be like baptism. Water and quick moving creek. Something powerful that rush over me say *this* what love feel like.

I got a dress made for me. All from things left over. Nothing tossed away. The only thing seem to be, shouldn't. Then come me.

BORN STRANGE

The child in the caul
carries her eyes over
to the dead woman who pushed
her back into the womb

says, *I'll remember you
when I'm big*

dead woman laughs
not surprised that
she's been seen,

*sho you
will*

THE OPENING[7]

Betsey leans in with sure hands
Lucy prepares for metal
slosh of seeping liquid

We are an unfortunate journey   a plunder
something to be found
something not to be seen

Introduce spoon and I am sacrament
unforgivable sin and reprieve   practiced
in the dark ghetto of my body

Something to master
something to enslave

Dear Lucy, dear Betsey, all of us
that we weren't so perfectly broken,
the scent of us so eagerly hunted,

if our mouths, when opened up
could light our darkness

BETSEY INVENTS THE SPECULUM
Fall 1845

Introducing the bent handle of the spoon I saw everything, as no man had ever seen before.
  —*from* The Story of My Life *by J. Marion Sims*

I have bent in other ways
to open the body   make space

More pliable than pewter,
my skin may be less giving

Great discoveries are made
on cushioned lessons and hard falls

Sims invents the speculum
I invent the wincing

the *if you must* of it
the looking away

the here of discovery

THE CALCULUS OF US

*"I spent a month very pleasantly in New Orleans, and got
acquainted with my friend Mr. P.T. Barnum, who was then
traveling with Jenny Lind and stopping in the same hotel with us."*
—*from* The Story of My Life *by J. Marion Sims*

Dear Joice,

My fate & yours,
an arithmetic.

Correct me if I'm wrong but:

*(f)*slave = canary
where canary means
recurring death

if this is true
you too were experiment
your exposed brain to my
contained urine

of these things
we are both cured

*(f)*cure = elimination
              preservation

there is honey in
never returning to fields
salt in 35 operations
your dissection
      subjection

*(f)*subject = conscious mind
              ego

autobiographical retraction
our ghosts, the stories

slippery abolitionist showman
coward confederate doctor

Treason of
the body is...

"*What might link a surgeon-slave-master to a showman-ringmaster? Both exercise mastery over bodies ...*"

    —Terri Kapsalis "Mastering the Female Pelvis"

SQUARE AND COMPASS, OR JOICE POSTHUMOUSLY REFLECTS ON THE GEOMETRY OF THE SHOWMAN'S RECOLLECTION

"I was favorably struck with the appearance of the old woman ... she was lying upon a high lounge in the middle of the room; her lower extremities were drawn up, with her knees elevated some two feet above the top of the lounge ..."
—*from* The Life Of P.T. Barnum, Written By Himself

I.
Square the right angle
between one leg that cannot move
one that will not

Bisect with
your horror

PROOF:
empty breasts
hungry mouths

2.
Diameter distance between
Boston and Alabama

PROOF:
bill of sale

3.
Find the radius to Anarcha
look legs first

PROOF:
Showman is doctor
doctor is showman

4.
Tangent this history

JOICE HETH PRESENTS:
THE SHOWMAN AS DENTIST[8]

When he starts on the incisor I think of the
time my first child was conceived,
white shirt against my face
oil on the back of my tongue.

It fills my mouth, I choke.
He pushes my head to spit.
His shoe soiled.
His fist loosens the next tooth.
I swallow it.

He must work for each of these.
Work as hard as they have to stay here.
Work as hard as I did to be beaten
before the boneless child passed as feces.

My face against his shirt
muddied with my blood
my spit.

Semen of ten shipmen
smell of broken virgins
oil on the back of my tongue.

Teeth collect in my lap
some broken and sharp on gums

If I bit down it would be
my own blood shed
My mouth stayed soft.
Soft, so I would not die

Showman whispers
satisfied,
My   black   beauty.

JOICE HETH CATALOGUES THE SKIN

Body has a way of moving on
without you. When the mind says
hold on, I finally got something right
body goes on, marks time.
Time and skin are my business.

Skin rarely lets me remember the good
so I make good memories for it.
One line for when I got born
grins across my belly
another crosses it, knows
what the skin has stretched to hold.

I prayed for it
in the back of my knee
smooth now   hallowed
to the touch.

JOICE HETH CONTEMPLATES THE WHALE IN PINOCCHIO OR HER RIGHT ARM

P.T. Barnum quotes "a visitor" in his memoirs, "Joice Heth is not a human being. What purports to be a remarkably old woman is simply a curiously constructed automaton, made up of whalebone, india-rubber, and numberless springs ingeniously put together, and made to move at the slightest touch, according to the will of the operator."

i.
Phineas,
you build me
without eyes as if
I'd find it easier
not to see you
make me or
george in my arm

sucking

sometimes, I forget that
I am not real and
long for a mouth
to stretch the skin

ii.
Pinocchio,
A dream:

I brush
against baleen and
wake up screaming

milk

It would be easier
if I could forget being real
one dead arm
cannot

Baby, my lies could
chop a cherry tree
I could use some
string

iii.
Visitor,
the slightest touch
is what puppets know
we also know

paralysis is made
by masters
who lay us down
indefinitely

I am not mortal
but what is the difference
between laying down
and dying?

BENEDICTION IN PROVIDENCE[9]

*"At the close of the service, the old lady [Joice Heth] commenced an
antiquated hymn ..."*
  —*from the* New York Baptist

I am the map unfurling   yet
I am at home
between the teeth of the beast

Priest-ridden saints partake
touch their hearts
eyes to the sky

I have never been religious
but truth is as clear
as a cannibal's smile

o, tearing bicuspids
o, hull of this terrible ship
o, my mis-direction

This is the way you feed them
heart first   they will
forget the rest

They pronounce it *antique*
cured meat
an abolitionist feast

Muddy baptismal waters
drink for them
virtue of shame

o, lost Moses
o, greatest show
o, my   tender flesh   gone

JOICE HETH NARRATES HER DISSECTION[10]
February 25, 1836

He thinks of the time he dissected a
human

> *the brain will take much force to reveal*

how he found hardness in her organs

> *tangible character*

Age does these things. It hardens us
to the air. Hardens us in our sin

> *luscious fatty meat.*

Hardens like the flesh of a thing that
saves time

> *Comparable to her fellow bondsmen*

I could be machine. Skull
notwithstanding—I'm suspicious

> *she was cared for*
> *death—for a vice.*

how my chest bristles. bends as a corset.

> *Heart is a hollow tomb*

I, industrious beast
beast of industry

    not this wet yielding
    thing she is all

a tin woman with a heart
beats a glorious ending

    lies

JOICE HETH PRESENTS: HERSELF!
February 19, 1836

AND FOR MY LAST TRICK
I WILL RELEASE THE GHOST
Hover over my corpse
and escape.

You will open her. DISCOVER
ancient black. OBSERVE
this DISAPPEARING ACT

Read her femur like rings
on a tree. *Count slow*
to 81 years

Pelvis tells you she had
children. WONDER
if she nursed them

NOTICE
a smirk of
knowing

Eyes sunk, dim.
WATCH
you

diminish
to life
size.

THE ART OF NOT DYING A SLAVE

The art of not dying a slave is
one for those who know the
lash to be a kiss on your will

Find your heaven on earth
mock your master and go there
tell the truth when you lie

Dream of something wondrous
claim you have no dream
Find a vice and stick to it

Die early   die old
Die with your head on his
feather pillows

LEST YOU FORGET[11]

I listen to what he holds
higher than himself

on the one-hundred-sixty-first day he reminisces about
how he shook The General's hand

I giggle
nearly spill his evening porridge.

amuse myself with a plausible addition
to his myth:

founding father, cheery tree, honest boy
my brown nipple in his lying mouth.

I listen deep
contrive my own telling

what he will remember
when he puffs up, thinks himself high

as his god: against black flesh
washington suckled

black hands clothed, held him
had mercy on his infant neck

THE RESEARCHER THINKS ON THE
IMMORTALITY OF JOICE HETH

It's like when I was told that Pluto was not a planet.
What lived light years in my mind was never there.
Darkness, it stays. What science giveth it taketh away.

Questions that linger:

Did she know?
Whose black tit did the general suck?
Why do I dream of dead babies pulling my breasts?

Parity

Approximately 50% of the specimen is submitted...
(from the Researcher's medical file)

PARITY

parity n. medicine. the fact or condition of having borne a specified number of children.

—Oxford English Dictionary

There might be something called an impatient.

Pregnancy tests, doctors' whispers, my week long funk, sterile lubricant, discarded speculums. Every wear of morphine mimics a familiar morning   another dream of drowning in mucous   meeting a dead ovary: She floats yellow. Spits ovum into the poison. Wrinkles black in mourning.

BEDSIDE MANNER

Pull from the arms

they will grow to
fill space.

Now twist

Note
the extension of spine
cracking hips

    extended toes

 hollow mouth

Pull again
hold the hands
now

unfold the fists.

ON THE POLITICS OF CITATION

Esmin Green[12] the thought that perhaps this is a metaphor for how we all die. Green an idea of metaphors that live where bodies cannot.

Some things were left when she died on that Kings County emergency room floor: her body and *who else?*

Open parentheses Green close parentheses. Her name now locked in line. The line is, *No one noticed.* It continues, *differentiate me from death.*

ORDER
for Esmin Green

To tuck oneself in the manner of
a fleeting day: flaking scalp
hair in a brush

To fold oneself neatly
and fall to the floor
to be dying

as is the natural order of things
to walk past   be annoyed even
how can we shed her from our lives?

how the spirit   sits upright in wait
how the mind   resolves its chores

GHOSTING

when the body holds the mind accountable orgasm
chill bitter **an innershift** cough   weep excite longing
when the tongue cannot know bursting   pimple
knows deeply skin salt rash slave lot's wife salt
keloid memory, someone else's memory, your
memory shame pulse fat blood tissue muscle
dehydrated **when the mind is a body** disease road
another kind of vessel tributaries   passage bowels
birth **& thought** head headache amnesia
a corpse. heart hand palm hosanna soul sou so

AN EXPERIMENT IN PATIENCE

Watch a seed
assemble a tree yielding
fully ripe peaches

It is not at all like
waiting for your children
to come home undead
or counting each nerve
exposed by a whip
it is not like your father
waiting in line for the shot
to his head

There are waits, sufferings
seemingly equal
Some, apparently, un-chosen
most unbearable
attentive waits
without respite from
reach

THE RESEARCHER CONTEMPLATES VENUS

When I talk about my work I am asked to speak of
Saartjie Baartman.

I take Saartjie's hand and ask her: *Where would you like
for me to put you?* She laughs, or maybe she sighs.
Researchers only ask leading questions. Questions that
lean toward the body sometimes trip over the dead.

WHEN ASKED, "WHERE DO YOU COME UP WITH THIS STUFF?"

Memories do not ask me to come. They fall into my head in the form of primary sources, block quotes, secondary theories and side-glances. As in: ...*so you know what that's about.*

Memories do not care for the politics of the day. Life begins before conception and ends in footnotes, underfunded research, and parentheticals. As in: *(others have shown us that race is not a unitary sign.)*

Memories do not wait for the word to bring them life. Instead they wake from mysterious sensations while I urinate, the episode of *Mystery Diagnosis*, a friend who sends me an instant message asking, *Have you heard of Henrietta Lacks?*

HAUNTED BY THE LIVING,
I TALK TO THE DEAD

who scrutinize my inadequate notes. Notes that could never contain the grave trampling of narrative. The "what has happened here"[13] of your life. The premium cable telling of it.

At first I thought I feared your eye, Mrs. Lacks. But now I realize it is the gaze of your loved ones. I should make monument to you. Instead, ~~it is as if~~ I am figuring my life through your death.

The living wake, stare at me. Sleep is disappearance. The safety of *there are no survivors.*

OF AIR AND SEA
for Henrietta Lacks, after Walcott

I have almost died four times

first in the womb
suffocating on the Idea

twice nearly drowned

once at Mount Sinai
lungs failing
chest compressing
extending

you were the science
so that I would not

you   on that last bed
you   in tubes growing
  all around

had I known
I would have wept
would not have thought
of death
myself

had not an autopsy
a fistula
your cells…

~

what lives would be uncradled?
what discoveries never proclaimed?
what bodies left between here
and oblivion?

all encompassing blue
vast open coffin
of air and sea

I am thankful for medicine
the way it cradles
kills

death isn't careless

breathing even
if difficult is air

air   not salt water
not yet

I do not want to be responsible
for the retelling

there is no returning
to mother's dreamless sleep

no heritage cruise
only forward

through the mind's
backward gaze

when there may be
some chance
of forgetting
mind veers off
to the waves

you are memory

you are everything

AT [THE TEACHING HOSPITAL]
FOR THE SECOND TIME
April 27, 2006

To each doctor a speculum.

No time for a room with walls.
No procedure. No apologies. No
apologies all mine.

I have not yet learned
how to look
when I am entered.

Not yet learned
where to turn.
Ceiling?
Curtain?
The barrel of
myself?

Or, to the patient beside me
who, in his sleep,
mumbles
i'm going nigger hunting,
i'm gon' get you, nigger.

FILL A WOMAN WITH MEANING

Look
uninhibited.
Children
the stroll
no lye relaxer.

Tell her
how to
rest her chin
wipe tears

when to
become woman
make love
never forget.

Explain to her
her sadness
fibroids,
miscarriage
blood sugar,
Welbutrin.

Bend a spoon
find the torn,
the growing,
find what separates
apes from men.

Whatever you do,
do not pull curtains
to primitive
night.

Do not shatter the
mirror to reveal
animal trainer
artist,
lover,
surgeon.

Do not let her know
terror
belongs to you.

HOW TO MEASURE PAIN II: MAGGOT BRAIN
Thanks to Funkadelic.

How do you daughter measure pain?
How do you suture a cracked skull flickering
South?

> One moment you are flying
> over North Carolina
> next you are eating red dirt
> screaming at someone's feet
> dangling

> > It's 1999
> > a chain snaps
> > a head rolls
> > it starts to rain

in your pelvis
they examine you,
you whimper
knees buckle

feet in stirrups
a gloved hand no
a bent spoon

stirring brimley
stew pot.

How do you, daughter, forget
dying in 1830-something?

Your hand in your dress trying to find the child
whose infant head is beneath a heel
It's 1917 and the smell
of gasoline is a lot like

gasoline

you fill your tank
drive home
stop in an
intersection
you cannot move
they honk

you stand

they prod
fondle

your breasts
in the mouth of a child
he is not yours

his face imprinted on the jar of food
turning in your hand
quick now, in your pocket.

Write this
down.

Don't forget

you are a good daughter.
you remember your
mothers' names.

You cry and you don't know why
in the library looking up *The Negro: A Beast*
pages open beneath hands
from 1970 to 2006

how do you, daughter
measure pain?

by the length and width
of your black woman self

echo of a scream
muffled
under cupped hands
in wild eyes
graceful nods
smiles

you have found yourself
in each broken body
each elation

your mother's scar
hers and
hers
and you.

A DIAGNOSIS IS AN ENDING

an intricate inconvenience
that comes on maybe
temporary

Cramps, a lump,
nothing but the body's
unreliability
its service to us
and itself
   present, robust
yet tied to an illusion

Nothing saves
nothing swings low
to the root

  only slows.
    Its shadow
               lengthens

A diagnosis is an ending
to the idea that
we are not human.

TO THE PATIENT

Tears will only leave
you wanting for water
and more time.
Which, as you know,
will be spent waiting.

ACKNOWLEDGMENTS

I am so grateful for the following publications that have previously published versions of the poems in this book.

"The Researcher Discovers Anarcha, Betsey, Lucy," and "On the Politics of Citation." *Meridians: Feminism, Race, Transnationalism* 11.2.2013.

"Benediction in Providence," *Cave Canem Anthology XII*, Willow Books, Detroit, MI. 2012.

"The Opening," *Aunt Chloe*. 2011.

"Joice Heth Catalogues the Skin," "Benediction in Providence," and "Joice Heth Presents: The Showman as Dentist." *Mythium Literary Magazine*. Spring 2010.

"Order" and "Square and Compass," *Torch: Poetry, Prose, and Short Stories by African American Women*. Spring/Summer 2010.

CREDITS

Lucille Clifton, excerpts from "why some people be made at me sometimes" and "shadows" from *The Collected Poems of Lucille Clifton*. Copyright © 1991, 1996 by Lucille Clifton. Reprinted with the permission of The Permissions Company, Inc., on behalf of BOA Editions Ltd., www.boaeditions.org.

The endnote to the poem "Negative Space Methodology" comes from *Ghostly Matters* by Avery Gordon and is used with the permission of the author.

The poem "Inner Truth" contains text from Rita Dove in an interview with Grace Cavalieri found in *The American Poetry Review*, and Elsa Barkley Brown in her essay "What Has Happened Here" found in *Feminist Studies*, volume 18, number 2 and are used with the permission of the author. The poem, "Haunted by the Living, I Talk to the Dead" also contains text from Barkley Brown's essay and is used with her permission.

Some text in the endnote to the poem "Etymology of Anarcha I" comes from Evelyn Hammonds' article "Black (W)holes and the Geometry of Black Female Sexuality" found in *differences: A Journal of Feminist Cultural Studies*, volume 6 issues 2+3 and is used with the permission of the author.

Text in the endnote to the poem "Lest You Forget" comes from Benjamin Reiss' *The Showman and the Slave* and is used with permission of the author.

The section "Treason of the Body is…" contains a quote from Terri Kapsalis' article "Mastering the Female Pelvis" found in

GRATITUDE

So many words of thanks to Diane Goettel and everyone at Black Lawrence Press for plucking this little project out of a heap and seeing its worth. To Cave Canem—I do not think that this project would have developed without the time, space, and instruction I received during all of my summers with you. To Khadijah Queen, Natasha Marin, Ashaki Jackson and Anastacia Tolbert especially for being a nest of wild creativity. Lynne Procope, L. Lamar Wilson, Phillip Williams and the whole CC family for cheering this project on. Carl Phillips, Ed Robeson, Cornelius Eady, Toi Derricotte, Claudia Rankine, Cyrus Cassells, Colleen McElroy and E. Ethelbert Miller for your careful eyes. Rachel Eliza Griffiths for your generosity and grace. Fred Joiner, Jon West Bey, Derrick Brown, Mahogany Browne and the folks at the Reginald F. Lewis Museum for creating opportunities for me to share this project.

To my mom and dad for your continued support of my craft and life. To the rest my family for continued support and love: Grandmother, the original poet in the family, Granddad, DaWayne, Aunt Faye, Uncle Keith, Aunt Katherine, Aunt Margaret, Vermonja thank you all for loving me through all of my many endeavors. To Elsa Barkley Brown, Michelle Rowley, Deborah Rosenfelt, Sheri Parks, Psyche Williams Forson, Ana Perez, Rajani Bhatia, Mel Lewis, Safoura Nourbakhsh and everyone in the Women's Studies and American Studies departments at the University of Maryland, thank you for seeing me.

To my dear friend Sarah Stefana Smith for always holding me accountable to craft. Ruby Sales for mentorship and instructing me to trust in art. Thank you Deborah McKinney, for being a big sis. WeMean, always. Always, the word. To Sharan Strange and Opal Moore, for seeing in me, a poet at the most crucial time. To a great mentor who lifted me out through poetry, who believed in me and my words, Jacqueline Jones Lamon. Thank you. Thank you. Thank you.

ENDNOTES

1. Avery Gordon on Patricia Williams in *Ghostly Matters: Haunting and the Sociological Imagination*. "This is a project where finding the shape described by her absence captures perfectly the paradox of the tracking through time and across all those forces that which makes its mark by being there and not there at the same time."

2. "I could go after an inner truth. That freed me." Rita Dove in an interview with Grace Cavalieri in *The American Poetry Review*, volume 24, number 2.

3. Elsa Barkley Brown in "'What Has Happened Here': The Politics of Difference in Women's History and Feminist Politics" in *Feminist Studies*, volume 18, number 2.

4. "She willingly consented," said Sims, "I... mounted her on the table, on her knees, with her head resting on the palms of her hands." From *The Story of My Life* by J. Marion Sims.

5. Anarcha and her child's condition upon Sim's first meeting her: "The child's head was so impacted in the pelvis that the labor pains had almost entirely ceased. It was evident that matters could not long remain in this condition without the system becoming exhausted, and without the pressure producing a sloughing of the soft parts of the mother." *The Story Of My Life* by J. Marion Sims.

6. "Black women's sexuality is often described in metaphors of speechlessness, space, or vision, as a 'void' or empty space that is simultaneously ever visible (exposed) and invisible and where black women's bodies are always already colonized." Evelyn Hammonds "Black (W)holes and the Geometry of Black Female Sexuality" in *differences: A Journal of Feminist Cultural Studies*, volume 6 issues 2+3.

7. J. Marion Sims "On The Treatment Of Vesico-Vaginal Fistula": "An assistant on each side lays a hand in the folds between the glutei muscles and the thigh, the ends of the fingers extending quite to the labia majora […] and then, by lifting the perineum, stretching the sphincter, and raising up the recto-vaginal septum, it is easy to view the whole vaginal canal as it is to examine the fauces by turning a mouth widely open, up to a strong light." *The American Journal of the Medical Sciences*, 1852.

8. In his memoir P.T. Barnum refers to Heth as his "black beauty."

9. Recollecting his time in Providence, Rhode Island, P.T. Barnum referred to the people there as "priest-ridden" and "under the anathemas of the clergy."

10. "An absence of ossification of the arteries in the immediate region of the heart was deemed by the dissector and most of the gentlemen present an evidence against the assumed age of Joice," reported Barnum in his memoir *The Life of P.T. Barnum, Written by Himself.*

11. "Could the career of the greatest entertainer of the nineteenth century have originated with a slave's subtle mockery of her master?" —Benjamin Reiss, *The Showman and the Slave.* I'd like to think so.

12. In 2008, Esmin Green waited for services at Kings County Hospital in New York for nearly twenty-four hours and died on the waiting room floor.

13. Elsa Barkley Brown "'What Has Happened Here': The Politics of Difference in Women's History and Feminist Politics."